SPACE BUSTERS

SPACE
ALIENS

Steve Parker

Raintree

Chicago, Illinois

LOOK FOR THE ALIEN

Look out for boxes like this with the alien in the corner. They contain extra information and amazing space-buster facts and figures.

Published by Raintree, a division of Reed Elsevier, Inc.

Designer: Tessa Barwick
Editors: Sarah Doughty, Pam Wells
Consultant: Stuart Atkinson

Library of Congress Cataloging-in-Publication Data
Parker, Steve.
    Space aliens / Steve Parker.
       p. cm.—(Space busters)
    Includes index.
    Summary: Describes the concept of alien beings, how they have been represented in our culture, and whether they may really exist.
       ISBN 0-7398-4849-6 (HC),
    1-4109-0072-X (Pbk.)
       1. Life on other planets—Juvenile literature. [I. Extraterrestrial beings.] I. Title. II. Series.

QB54 .P34 2002
576.8'39—dc21   2001041729

Printed in Hong Kong.
Bound in the United States.
1 2 3 4 5 6 7 8 9 0 LB 05 04 03 02 01

Acknowledgments
We wish to thank the following individuals and organizations for their help and assistance and for supplying material in their collections: Camera Press back cover top (Lucasfilm Ltd), 5 bottom (Lucasfilm Ltd), 6 left (Luc Hieulle), 16 top (W Drommer), 16 bottom (Lucasfilm Ltd), 21 bottom (Jerry Watson), 23 bottom, 27 (Tom Keller); Corbis back cover bottom left (Forrest J Ackerman Collection), 4 (Bettmann), 7 (Forrest J Ackerman Collection), 13 bottom, 17 (Bettmann), 22 (George Hall), 25 left (Richard Cummins), 26 (L Clarke); Kobal Collection 18 (Peter Mayhew); MPM Images 3, 10, 11 centre, 11 bottom, 14, 28, 29; NASA 23 top; Science Photo Library front cover (Peter Menzel), back cover bottom right (Stuart Painter), 3 (Peter Menzel), 5 top (Stuart Painter), 8 left (Peter Menzel), 9 (Magrath/Folsom), 11 top (Peter Menzel), 12 (Julian Baum), 13 top (David A Hardy), 15 (A Gragera/Latin Stock), 19 top (Biophoto Associates), 24 (Victor Habbick Visions), 25 right (NASA); Topham Picturepoint 1, 6 right, 8 right, 19 bottom, 20, 21 top, 30.

◀ Some people believe that an alien, like this model, arrived at Roswell, New Mexico, in 1947.

▶ Must aliens have a head, body, arms, and legs? Perhaps a space being could look like a wispy cloud.

T 83389

Contents

WHAT ARE ALIENS?

A space alien is someone or something that is not from planet Earth, the world we know. A space alien comes from a strange and faraway place. So does this mean space aliens exist? Millions of people say that they do because they believe they have seen them.

Some people claim to have seen aliens and their spacecraft here on Earth. Others say that aliens have spoken to them, touched them, and even taken them for trips in their spacecraft. Most scientists say that there could be aliens, far out in space. But no one can prove this. So the best answer to the question "Are there aliens?" is "We don't know."

◀ Aliens in films and books have bulging brains, bug eyes, and clawed hands. This one, called Mutant, is from the planet Metaluma and starred in the 1955 film *This Island Earth*.

This does not keep people from wondering about aliens. What would they look like, and what powers would they have? Each year many stories, comic-strips, films, cartoons, and advertisements include aliens. They give us lots of ideas about what aliens might be like.

▲ Head, nose, eyes, mouth, neck—many aliens have all the body parts that we have. But they are made to look much weirder.

 ## ARE ALIENS ALIVE?

If we found an alien from another world, how would we tell it was alive? On Earth creatures eat food. They move about and detect their surroundings using senses such as sight and hearing. They grow up and breed to make more of their kind. Would an alien do all this?

▶ Two characters from the *Star Wars* movies are C3PO and R2D2. But they are machines, like robots, rather than living things. So are they aliens?

ALIENS IN THE PAST

▼ The temple of Angkor Wat, in Cambodia, was built more than 600 years ago. It is so huge that people wondered whether aliens helped build it.

How long have aliens been around? Do any clues exist today from ancient times? Thousands of years ago, people made pictures on rocks and in caves. Some of the pictures seem to show strange beings coming down from the sky. But each one could easily be a person on a hill, or a chief on a throne.

▼ This rock art made thousands of years ago by Aboriginal, the earliest people in Australia could show a strange animal—or an alien!

Tales from long ago tell of powerful beings with magical powers. They could fly, throw lightning, take over people's minds, and disappear. Again, these stories are exciting, but they are not really proof of aliens.

In the U.S. in 1938, the radio news said that aliens from Mars were invading Earth! Listeners ran into the street in panic. In fact, it was actor Orson Welles reading make-believe news. The story was *The War of the Worlds*, written in 1898 by H.G. Wells. The radio announcer had to tell people that it was not a real invasion. But this shows how quick people are to believe in aliens.

▲ Martians moved in walking machines on stilt legs. They attacked Earth with heat rays in the book *The War of the Worlds*, written by H.G. Wells.

 ## OUR FAVORITE ALIENS

Around the year 1900, space scientist Percival Lowell believed that clever creatures lived on Mars. Through a telescope, he could see straight lines on the surface of the planet. He said these were canals built by Martians to carry water. But the "canals" were tricks of the light. Even so, Martians have been popular aliens ever since.

WHO HAS SEEN ALIENS?

▼ Did aliens land near Roswell, New Mexico, in 1947? Many people said that alien bodies were discovered and then studied by scientists.

Millions of people claim to see aliens. Almost every week, there is a report about them somewhere in the world. Why does this happen? And why are the aliens seen but never found or captured?

Some parts of the world have more reports of aliens than other parts. In some regions, people know about the idea of aliens. So the reports of sightings make regular news. Yet in other places, people know little about aliens, and there are hardly any sightings. Does this mean that aliens choose to visit some places on Earth and not others? Or does it mean that people who read reports about aliens are more likely to imagine seeing them?

▲ Rosalind Reynolds said that she was captured by aliens. Here she shows a picture of what they looked like.

Every few years, a film about aliens becomes popular. Soon after, more people than usual claim to see aliens. Often, the alien they see is similar to the alien in the film. Again, they may imagine that they have really seen what they saw in the film.

▲ An alien spacecraft? No, it's a cloud in the sky over Hawaii. Clouds with this saucerlike shape form naturally near mountains.

When one person claims to see an alien, this could be a trick of the light or their imagination. But sometimes many people see the same alien, all at the same time. These are called mass sightings and are much more difficult to explain.

 ALIEN DREAMS

Sometimes a dream seems real, especially if a person is tired or under stress. Some sightings of aliens could happen when people fall asleep for a moment, then wake up. They do not realize that they have simply had a dream.

WHERE ARE ALIENS?

The Moon has no air, no food, and no surface water. So astronauts did not expect to find aliens there.

Humans have certain needs. These needs include water to drink, food to eat, air to breathe, and heat to warm our bodies. Most of these things are made possible by light and heat from the Sun. If aliens lived in a similar way to us, they would have similar needs.

It is unlikely that aliens would float around in space, with no air, food, or water. And a star like the Sun would be much too hot to live on. So aliens might live on a planet, like Earth, or on a moon that revolves around a planet.

LOOKING FOR MARTIANS

Of all the planets, Mars is most similar to Earth. It has air, which is made up of a mixture of gases. Several space probes have landed on Mars and sent back photographs. They include *Vikings 1* and *2* in 1976 and the Mars *Pathfinder* in 1997. They found no aliens. But humans have not given up hope of finding some kind of life on Mars.

▲ Aliens might survive under giant domes that would protect them against dangerous rays.

The nearest world to us is the Moon. It has no air or water on its surface. Also, space probes (unmanned spacecraft) and astronauts have visited the Moon and have found no trace of aliens on its rocky surface.

Earth is one of nine planets that go around the Sun. Space probes have been to all of these planets. Several planets have poisonous gases or burning heat that would kill life instantly. Probes have sent back pictures and information from the other planets. But they have found no aliens.

▲ It would take thousands of our lifetimes to reach deep space.

If aliens do exist, they must be much farther away. It could take hundreds or even thousands of years to reach them.

▼ The planet Venus is covered by choking clouds and burning fumes. They would kill anything that lived like we do.

ALIEN CRAFT

When we want to travel a long way, we go by car, train, plane, or ship. If aliens wanted to travel long distances, they too would choose a good spacecraft to travel in—a spaceship. Many people claim that they have seen alien spacecraft.

A mysterious object moving through the air is called a UFO, which stands for **u**nidentified **f**lying **o**bject. People have described hundreds of different UFOs. Some glow with lights, move incredibly fast, make no sound, and appear or disappear suddenly. There are also many photographs of UFOs.

Usually, there is some explanation for a UFO. It might be a plane, airship, or balloon. It could be a rocket or satellite something that travels around a planet. Then, it would pass low over Earth. It may be unusual weather, such as lightning or a cloud with a strange shape.

◄ In 1987 many people around Belleville, Wisconsin, saw various strange craft. This is a drawing of a rod-shaped one with lights.

Alien craft may appear suddenly out of a "wormhole." This is like an invisible tunnel through space. But no one knows if wormholes exist.

Some photographs of UFOs are tricks or fakes. They are usually made by people who try to trick others in order to become rich or famous.

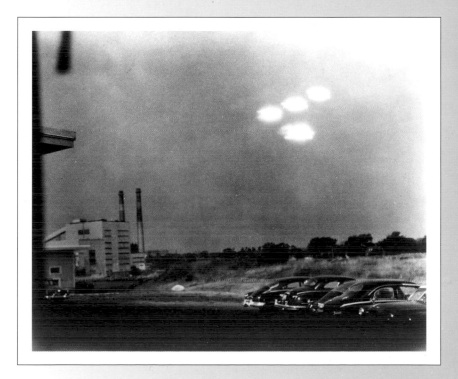

SECRET SIGHTS

During the 1950s and 60s there were many UFO claims. This was a time of great rivalry between two powerful countries, the U.S. and U.S.S.R. (Russia and other members of the union). Each tried to build better planes, rockets, and missiles. Many UFOs could have been secret military aircraft.

This photograph shows glowing UFOs over a parking lot in Salem, Massachusetts. It was taken in 1952. At that time there was a great interest in UFOs and alien movies.

WHAT ALIENS WANT

Just suppose that aliens are super-clever, with amazing and advanced spacecraft. Even so, it would take a huge effort to travel across the vastness of space. If they could do this, why would aliens take the trouble to come to a tiny, backward world like Earth?

▲ An exploding star may threaten a distant world where aliens live.

We do not know. Perhaps their homes are too crowded or they need food or fuel. Perhaps their world is dying. It could have been hit by a lump of space rock, or struck by dangerous rays when a nearby star exploded. Or maybe they do not need anything from us but would like to take over our Earth?

Many times in history, people have tried to conquer other people and take over their lands. Powerful, warlike aliens might do the same with planets. We could become their slaves. On the other hand, aliens could be kind and friendly. They might see how we are damaging our own world, with wars, starvation, and pollution. They might come here to help.

BREAKDOWN!

Even the best alien spaceship could break down. If this happened near the Earth, the aliens might stop here to make repairs. But they might not like Earth at all. They could be frightened by busy, noisy, clumsy Earthlings. Maybe they would repair their craft in secret and leave as soon as possible!

▼ One day, we might dig rocks from space to use here on Earth. Aliens could come to Earth for the same reason—to use valuable resources.

THE SHAPE OF ALIENS

Imagine an alien. Does it have a head, a body, two arms, and two legs? Many aliens in films and books and on television look very similar to human beings. But think of how many different living things there are on Earth. Is there any reason why aliens should be like us?

No. The general humanlike shape is called "humanoid." We often imagine aliens to have humanoid shapes. But for life here on Earth, apart from humans, the humanoid shape is very rare. Most creatures have four legs like dogs and cats, or six legs like insects.

▲ Neelix, from *Star Trek Voyager*, is almost like a human. He came from Rinax, a moon of the planet Talax.

▶ Jabba from *Star Wars* has a fat face like a human, but his body is like a giant slug!

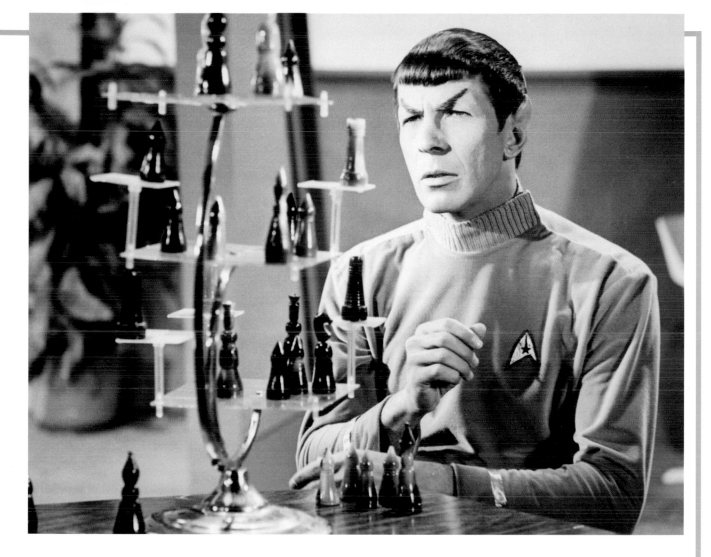

There is no reason for aliens to have any legs. They could be almost any shape we can imagine. In films and on television, many aliens are shaped like people because they are human actors with costumes and makeup. This is easier than inventing a new type of creature with a very strange, unfamiliar shape.

▲ *Star Trek's* **Mr. Spock is recognized by his pointed ears. All people from his world, Vulcan, have them.**

ALIEN TALK

In stories about aliens, they usually speak our languages. But there is no reason why aliens should be able to speak like us. It happens mainly so that we can understand what the aliens say. If there really are aliens, they might communicate in a very different way, such as by flashes of light. It could be very difficult for us to understand them.

ANIMAL-LIKE ALIENS

Think of some aliens you have seen recently—on television, in films, in books, and comics. Some are shaped like creatures on Earth. Birds, worms, ants, monkeys, dinosaurs—famous make-believe aliens look like all of these creatures.

Yet there is no reason why real aliens should look like Earth animals. They might be totally different in shape and even in size. An alien could be as big as a mountain or as small as a pea. It might be pure energy, like a wispy cloud.

◄ In *Star Wars*, Chewbacca is a type of alien called a Wookie. He, or it, is shaped like a huge gorilla.

Why do make-believe aliens often look like animals? One reason is that it helps us to recognize the aliens and understand their actions. We know something about the behavior of monkeys. So when a monkey-shaped alien jumps up and down and screeches, we guess that it is angry or frightened. This helps us to follow the story.

▲ A terrifying alien from planet Zog? No, a grain weevil from planet Earth! This tiny beetle would fit into this "o".

◄ Worms may look creepy, but they are just ordinary animals. The hydra lives in ponds.

GOOD OR BAD ALIENS

Imagine if aliens really exist. What would they be like? Would they be good or bad? Would they be friendly or frightening? When aliens appear on television and in movies, some are nice while others are evil.

Stories that feature aliens are known as science fiction. They can be exciting adventures, where anything can happen. There might be amazing aliens in incredible spacecraft from faraway worlds, fighting ghosts from the past and future. The only limit is our imagination.

▶ Ahh! ET the alien is from the movie *ET The Extra-Terrestrial*. He, or it, is cute and kind and gentle.

Many of these aliens seem to know the difference between right and wrong. The bad aliens are often ugly and mean. In the stories, they usually come off worse. The good aliens are honest, strong, and brave, and they usually win over the bad aliens. We like this because it appeals to our sense of right and wrong.

▼ Ugh! Martians in the movie *Mars Attacks* are horrible, fierce, and deadly—yet quite funny!

But there is no reason why this should be so. On a far-off planet, deep in space, aliens could behave in a totally different way. They might not even have any sense of right and wrong.

UNFEELING ALIENS

A machine has no thoughts or feelings. It cannot be happy or sad. Aliens might be the same. They could be very clever, able to build starships and cross the universe. But their minds could be unfeeling, like computers. We would find this difficult to understand.

◄ In the movie *Independence Day*, warlike aliens try to take over Earth and kill millions of people.

▲ High-flying aircraft listen for radio signals and other messages that might come from aliens nearing Earth.

SEARCH FOR ALIENS

Scientists are searching for aliens all the time. They use giant telescopes to detect rays, waves, and signals coming from space. If the signals go on and off in a code, they could be messages sent by aliens.

SETI is the Search for Extra-Terrestrial Intelligence. Extra-Terrestrial means "beyond our planet." Huge telescopes around the world receive light rays, radio waves, and other waves. These have traveled billions of miles through space. Computers scan the signals. They look for patterns and codes that could be messages from aliens.

A FALSE ALARM

In 1967, scientists found strange bursts of radio waves from space. The waves went beep-beep-beep all the time. Some people thought aliens were trying to get in touch with us. But scientists worked out that the radio signals came from stars known as pulsars. They spin around very fast and send out pulses of radio waves.

◀ Pulsars are small, old, heavy stars that spin very fast. Some send out many radio waves every second. Others pulse more slowly, every few seconds.

So far, SETI has found no signals that might be sent by aliens. But we have been looking for only a few dozen years. Compared to the time that the universe has existed, this is a very brief time.

▶ The Arecibo telescope, in Puerto Rico, is 1,000 feet (305 m) across. It picks up very faint waves from space and is used by SETI.

23

ARE ALIENS OUT THERE?

▲ An imaginary alien craft approaches Earth.

Most scientists agree that alien life could exist on planets like our own. For many years, no one knew if other stars, like our Sun, have planets. But in the past few years many planets have been found, going around distant stars. This makes alien life more likely.

The fastest possible speed we know is the speed of light. But space is vast. Even at the speed of light, it takes thousands of years for radio waves to cross a tiny corner of space. So any messages we get from aliens may have been sent thousands of years ago.

Aliens could be super-clever, able to send out incredibly powerful messages and travel in starships. They might find a way to go faster than light. On the other hand, aliens could be tiny blobs of jelly, with no intelligence at all.

But Earth scientists have not yet found aliens. Are they really out there? The answer is still "We don't know."

MICRO-ALIENS?

In 1996 some scientists said that they had found aliens! A lump of rock from Mars, called a meteorite, had fallen to Earth. It had tiny sausagelike shapes in it, 100 times thinner than human hairs. Some scientists said that these were Martian microbes (tiny living things), preserved as fossils. Others said that they were natural bits of rock, not formed by living things.

▼ Were these tiny objects once alive, on planet Mars?

◀ In *Star Trek*, the Borg travel through space and time, taking over everything they meet.

Space Alien Facts

Here are some interesting facts and figures about space and aliens.

No proof yet
Every year there are hundreds of claims about seeing, hearing, and contacting aliens. Even so, there is no certain, definite, complete scientific proof that aliens exist or have visited us. No one has ever captured an alien for the world to see and study.

▲ One day, a strange spacecraft may really land on Earth, and aliens might come out. It would be the biggest news story of all time.

Early sightings
In Ancient Rome, some 1,600 years ago, a writer, Julius Obsequens, described "things like ships seen in the sky" and "a round object like a globe or circular shield that took its path in the sky." Were these early UFO sightings?

Flying saucers
In June 1947, pilot Kenneth Arnold was flying a small plane near Mount Rainier, near Ashford, Washington. He described nine objects, each "flat like a pie pan and so shiny it reflected the sun like a mirror," flying at incredible speed.

Strange lights
Many people reported seeing patterns of lights around Lubbock, Texas, in 1951. Photographs were taken and the objects were tracked by radar, but they were never properly explained.

On film
In 1978 UFOs were not only watched, but also photographed, taped, filmed, and tracked on radar for the first time, near the South Island of New Zealand. But some scientists said they were easily explained in various ways.

Alien HQ

The most famous UFO story is from Roswell in New Mexico, where a UFO is supposed to have crashed in 1947. UFO enthusiasts say that several aliens were rescued from the wreckage, and taken to a secret military base to be studied. Some people think they may still be alive today….

SETI telescopes

Scientists have searched vast regions of space, but no signals from aliens have been found. They use many telescopes including the world's largest, Arecibo, in Puerto Rico.

Aliens on the big screen

Every year there are several big films about space and aliens. You may have heard of some of them, or even seen them.

- The *Star Wars* series of films has hundreds of kinds of aliens.
- The *Star Trek* series of television programs and films, and the spin-offs, like *Next Generation, Voyager,* and *Deep Space Nine,* all feature aliens.
- The film *Stargate* shows how a doorway or "portal" across space and time can lead into an alien world.
- *Independence Day* is a spectacular film where aliens try to destroy Earth's cities, but American heroes stop them.

▲ Many people are afraid of the unknown. Others like to dress up and pretend! There are many clubs for fans of *Star Wars, Star Trek,* and the Roswell aliens (above).

- *ET The Extra-Terrestrial* is a film about one of the cutest aliens. This alien had baby features such as a big head, large eyes, a tubby body, and a toddler's walk, so that everyone would love it.
- The film *Close Encounters of the Third Kind* traces how alien craft are detected. Then, the aliens land so that they can meet us.

SPACE ALIEN WORDS

alien (AY-lee-uhn)
A space alien is someone or something that is not from our world, planet Earth.

astronaut (AS-truh-nawt)
The name for someone who has traveled into space.

**Extra-Terrestrial
(ek-Struh-tuh-RESS-tree-uhl)**
This means "beyond our planet"—not from Earth. Also the shortened version, ET, is the popular name of a famous alien. This alien wanted to "go home."

humanoid (HYOO-muhn-oid)
Shaped like a human with a head, an upright body, and two arms and two legs.

invasion (in-VAY-shuhn)
When one group of living things comes into or enters the place of another group, and tries to take over.

▶ **Planet Jupiter has many moons. Could one have aliens on it?**

moon
An object that goes around, or orbits, a planet. Our own planet, Earth, has one moon, which we call the Moon. Mars has two moons, and other planets have up to 15 or more.

planet (PLAN-it)
An object that goes around, or orbits, a star. Our own star, the Sun, has nine planets, making up the Solar System. Earth is the third planet from the Sun.

pulsar (PUHL-sar)
An old, small, heavy, fast-spinning star, also called a neutron star. It sends out regular bursts or pulses of radio waves.

SETI
Search for **E**xtra-**T**errestrial **I**ntelligence. This is the quest to find life forms that are quite clever and form societies or civilizations. Perhaps they even travel into space—just as humans do from here on Earth.

▲ Perhaps one of our space probes will find signs of life, or even real alien beings, on a distant world.

sighting (SITE-ing)
When people see, or think they see, an alien or an alien spacecraft or a strange, unexplained event.

space
Everywhere that is not Earth. Most of space is indeed empty space. It is dotted with tiny specks that are stars and other objects.

spacecraft/spaceship (kraft)
A craft or vehicle that can carry people into space.

space probe (prohb)
A machine or device for exploring space, that does not carry people. It is controlled by information usually sent as radio signals from Earth. It sends back signals about what it has found.

speed of light
The distance that light travels in a certain time. It is about 186,000 miles (115,580 km) in one second.

star
An object in space that shines with incredibly hot, burning gases. A star gives off light, heat, and many types of rays and waves.

telescope (TEL-uh-skope)
A device that makes faraway objects look nearer and bigger, showing more of their details. For example, optical telescopes work using light rays and show pictures. Radio telescopes detect radio waves.

UFO
Unidentified Flying Object. An object in the sky or the air that cannot be explained, in the normal way, as a plane, balloon, rocket, cloud, satellite, or lightning.

universe (YOO-nuh-vurss)
Everything there is—all of space, stars, planets, galaxies, and everything else. It includes all the things we know about, and even all the things we can only imagine.

USSR
A huge country in Europe and Asia that existed from 1917 to 1991, when it broke up into much smaller parts, such as Russia. From the 1950s until the 1970s the USSR was the main world rival to the U.S.

SPACE ALIEN PROJECTS

◀ This is a common type of alien picture. It was drawn by someone who claims to have been captured by aliens. Try to design something different.

DESIGN AN ALIEN

Draw some pictures of aliens and their spacecraft. Then study them as if you were a scientist. Do they look like people or any animals on Earth? How big are they? What do they eat, and how do they behave? Draw a picture of where they live, too. Make up an adventure story about them.

▶ Are these aliens friends or enemies? How can you tell?

MAGIC POWERS

Arthur C. Clarke, famous scientist and writer, suggested that if aliens really visited Earth, they would be so clever and advanced compared to us, that their powers would seem like magic. Imagine that you went back in time 150 years with a mobile phone. Could you explain how it worked to people who had never seen televisions, radios, or phones of any kind?

JOIN THE SEARCH

There are thousands, if not millions, of sites on the Internet about space, aliens, and SETI—the Search for Extra-Terrestrial Intelligence, far away in the universe. Some sites are fun, some are serious. There are several SETI groups in addition to the SETI Institute based in California. Hundreds of scientists are now working on SETI-type projects. The Internet is the place for the latest news and views.

SPACE ALIENS ON THE WEB

These are just some of the websites with information about the universe, aliens, and SETI.

SETI Institute Online

www.seti-inst.edu/Welcome.html

The home for scientific and educational projects about life in the universe. There are huge amounts of information about the latest developments in the science of SETI, the people who are considering how life began on Earth and whether life ever existed (or still exists) on other moons and planets.

Alien Explorer

www.alienexplorer.com

A science website for young people, using a science-fiction theme. You can play games, create your own aliens, and read stories.

Nova Online—Hunt for Alien Worlds

www.pbs.org/wgbh/nova/worlds

A large website with pages on the likelihood of alien life, where aliens might live, what they could look like, star maps, and other information.

SETI@Home—The Search for Extra-Terrestrial Intelligence

http://setiathome.ssl.berkeley.edu

A scientific experiment that uses computers linked to the Internet to help in the search for extra-terrestrial intelligence.

The Planetary Society—SETI page

http://seti.planetary.org

This society helps to set up and fund projects in the search for extra-terrestrial signals from other civilizations in the universe. Most projects scan the skies for radio and light signals from across the galaxy.

CSETI homepage

www.cseti.com

CSETI is the Center for the Study of Extra-Terrestrial Intelligence, founded in 1990. Its purpose is to make peaceful and long-term links with extra-terrestrial life forms, to educate, and to do scientific research.

UFO and Aliens News

http://aliens.phatstart.com

A fun site where you can read about the latest reports of UFO and alien "sightings." See pictures of Area 51 and other famous alien invasion sites.

You can search for information about distant planets, moons, stars, and galaxies by using an Internet search engine. Just type in the name of the subject you are looking for.

INDEX